Motive Power Review

£350

CW00819254

BOOK
THE
FIFTIES

BRITISH RAIL
CLASS 50's

John Chalcraft
and
Graham Scott-Lowe

PETER WATTS
Publishing

Copyright 1979

Published in Great Britain by
Peter Watts
13/15 Stroud Road
Gloucester
GL1 5AA

ISBN 0 906025 10 9

First printed 1979.
Re-printed 1983

Printed by Printflow
60-65 Redcliffe Street
Bristol BS1 6LS

Front Cover: 50046 'Ajax' passes Bridgwater with a down NE/SW route
express 1/6/82 (John Chalcraft)

Complete with 'Revenge' nameplates, but with its double-arrow symbol still
positioned centrally on its bodysides 50020 commences the climb to Rattery as it
leaves Totnes with the 07.30 Paddington-Penzance service, 31st August 1978.
(Graham Scott-Lowe)

Nameplate and crest of 50050 Fearless.

INTRODUCTION

Introduced in late 1967 these 2700 hp locomotives have, in a comparatively short period, lived a varied life on British Rail.

Originally numbered D400 – D449 and designated Type 4, they were allocated to Crewe for the sole purpose of powering trains over the (at that time) unelectrified section of the W.C.M.L. northwards from Crewe to Glasgow. However, when this project was completed the now reclassified Class '50's' were rapidly re-employed away from the L.M. to the Western Region, the first loco to arrive being D400, which started crew training in the Bristol area in October 1972. The newcomers were given a decidedly cool reception by loco crews and enthusiasts alike. Many of the '50's' arrived at their W.R. depots in a sorry, rather run down state and enthusiasts saw them as a distinct threat to their highly popular class 52 'Westerns'.

The story of the successful take over by the 'Hoovers', and the ultimate demise of the hydraulics is now, of course, history and one which has been chronicled in many other publications.

Slowly but surely the '50's' gathered popularity, partly due to the introduction by the Western Region of the even less glamorous H.S.T. units, but mainly due to B.R.'s commendable decision to heed the requests of many and bestow the entire fleet with names, and designating them 'Warship' class, reviving earlier W.R. diesel practice.

The early technical problems seem to have been ironed out by the Laira and Old Oak Common fitters and the 'Warships' have settled down to give sterling service.

Since 1979 class members have been through a modification programme when in Doncaster Works for general overhauls and have been returned to the Western Region in a modified livery since 50023 in 1980.

Though the majority of the class are based at Plymouth members can be seen throughout the W.R. system on a variety of duties, also straying onto the Midland region with South West – North West/East services, and the Southern in charge of the Waterloo – Exeter timetable.

What the future holds for the '50's' nicknamed 'Hoovers', remains a great mystery whilst the British Rail Board mull over the problem of whether to keep H.S.T.'s on the London – West of England route; certainly two other Regions have laid claim to the class if they cannot justify their presence in the West.

50001 (D401)   6th May, 1978   Whiteball
'Dreadnought'   (John Chalcraft)

50002 (D402)   2nd April, 1978   Bristol
'Superb'   (Graham Scott-Lowe)

| 50003 (D403)
'Temeraire' | 17th June, 1979 | Doncaster Works
(John Chalcraft) |
| 50004 (D404)
'St. Vincent' | 29th August, 1978 | Teignmouth
(Graham Scott-Lowe) |

| 50005 (D405) **'Collingwood'** | 23rd June, 1979 | Teignmouth (John Chalcraft) |

| 50006 (D406) **'Neptune'** | 13th November, 1976 | Birmingham New Street (Kevin Connolly) |

| 50007 (D407) | 10th June, 1978 | Dainton Bank |
| 'Hercules' | | (John Chalcraft) |

| 50008 (D408) | 27th January, 1979 | Cardiff Central |
| 'Thunderer' | | (Graham Scott-Lowe) |

50009 (D409)   13th May, 1978   Clink Road Junction
'Conqueror'   (John Chalcraft)

50010 (D410)   20th May, 1978   Whiteball
'Monarch'   (John Chalcraft)

| 50011 (D411) | 25th June, 1979 | St. Austell |
| 'Centurion' | | (John Chalcraft) |

| 50012 (D412) | 29th April, 1978 | Paignton |
| 'Benbow' | | (Graham Scott-Lowe) |

50013 (D413)	6th May, 1978	Taunton
'Agincourt'		(John Chalcraft)
50014 (D414)	19th June, 1978	Gloucester
'Warspite'		(Graham Scott-Lowe)

| 50015 (D415) | 26th May, 1979 | near Taunton |
| 'Valiant' | | (John Chalcraft) |

| 50016 (D416) | 23rd September, 1978 | Frome |
| 'Barham' | | (John Chalcraft) |

50017 (D417)   20th May, 1978   Bristol
'Royal Oak'   (John Chalcraft)

50018 (D418)   27th June, 1979   Bodmin Road
'Resolution'   (John Chalcraft)

50019 (D419)   10th June, 1978   Stoneycombe
'Ramillies'   (John Chalcraft)

50020 (D420)   30th September, 1978   Bristol
'Revenge'   (John Chalcraft)

50021 (D421)	23rd September, 1978	Bristol
'Rodney'		(John Chalcraft)
50022 (D422)	10th June, 1978	Dainton
'Anson'		(John Chalcraft)

| 50023 (D423) 'Howe' | 21st May, 1978 | Bristol (John Chalcraft) |

| 50024 (D424) 'Vanguard' | 31st March, 1979 | Plymouth (John Chalcraft) |

had the distinction of heading the last down locomotive hauled
'Riviera' seen here at Stoneycombe Quarry
9 'Implacable' on 5th August, 1979. (John Chalcraft)

50025 (D425)
'Invincible'

29th July, 1978

Frome
(John Chalcraft)

50026 (D426)
'Indomitable'

8th August, 1978

Old Oak Common
(Graham Scott-Lowe)

| 50027 (D427) | 6th May, 1978 | Taunton |
| **'Lion'** | | (John Chalcraft) |

| 50028 (D428) | 20th March, 1979 | Gloucester |
| **'Tiger'** | | (John Chalcraft) |

50029 (D429)   26th December, 1978   Paddington
'Renown'   (Graham Scott-Lowe)

50030 (D430)   25th June, 1979   St. Austell
'Repulse'   (John Chalcraft)

| 50031 (D431) | 30th August, 1978 | Plymouth |
| **'Hood'** | | (Graham Scott-Lowe) |

| 50032 (D432) | 29th June, 1979 | Bodmin Road |
| **'Courageous'** | | (John Chalcraft) |

| 50033 (D433) | 28th August, 1978 | Exeter |
| 'Glorious' | | (Graham Scott-Lowe) |

| 50034 (D434) | 28th October, 1978 | Paddington |
| 'Furious' | | (John Chalcraft) |

50035 (D435)   18th September, 1978   Gloucester
'Ark Royal'   (Graham Scott-Lowe)

50036 (D436)   5th November, 1978   Old Oak Common
'Victorious'   (Graham Scott-Lowe)

50037 (D437)   8th August, 1978   Old Oak Common
'Illustrious'   (Graham Scott-Lowe)

50038 (D438)   27th August, 1978   Newton Abbot
'Formidable'   (Graham Scott-Lowe)

| 50039 (D439) | 6th January, 1979 | Bristol |
| 'Implacable' | | (Graham Scott-Lowe) |

| 50040 (D440) | 25th October, 1978 | Paddington |
| 'Leviathan' | | (John Chalcraft) |

50041 (D441)	26th May, 1979	Reading
'Bulwark'		(John Chalcraft)
50042 (D442)	31st March, 1979	Penzance
'Triumph'		(John Chalcraft)

| 50043 (D443) | 24th June, 1979 | Westbury |
| **'Eagle'** | | (Graham Scott-Lowe) |

| 50044 (D444) | 14th May, 1978 | Westbury |
| **'Exeter'** | | (John Chalcraft) |

50045 (D445)		
'Achilles'	28th April, 1978	Bristol
		(John Chalcraft)
50046 (D446)	5th November, 1978	Old Oak Common
'Aiax'		(Graham Scott-Lowe)

| 50047 (D447)
'Swiftsure' | 29th August, 1978 | Dawlish – Teignmouth
(Graham Scott-Lowe) |
| 50048 (D448)
'Dauntless' | 23rd April, 1978 | Bristol
(John Chalcraft) |

50049 (D449)   28th August, 1978   Exeter
'Defiance'   (Graham Scott-Lowe)

50050 (D400)   2nd September, 1978   Castle Cary
'Fearless'   (John Chalcraft)

TECHNICAL DETAILS

Introduced 1967 – 1968
Built English Electric Co. Ltd, Vulcan Foundry, Newton-le-Willows, Lancs.
Wheel arrangement Co-Co
Engine English Electric 16 cylinder 16 CSVT
b.h.p. 2700 at 850 r.p.m.
Transmission 6 English Electric axle hung nose suspended 400 hp traction motors
Max. tractive effort 48,500 lb
Max. speed 100 m.p.h. (reduced to 95 m.p.h. from October 1982)
Axle loading limit 19 ton 10 cwt
Weight in working order 115 ton
Route availability 6
Height 12ft 9ins
Width 8ft 10ins
Length 68ft 6ins

This book forms part of the 'Motive Power Review' library, a series recording pictorially each locomotive within their British Rail class. Published so far are:

Book of the Forties
Book of the Peaks I (44's)
Book of the Peaks II (46's)
Book of the Peaks III (45/0's)
Book of the Fifties
Book of the Westerns (52's)
Book of the Deltics (55's)
Book of the Seventy-Sixes

Please write to the publisher for a complete list of current titles.

50044 'Exeter' is classically framed from within the goods shed at Lostwithiel on 27th June, 1979.
(John Chalcraft)